Commandant's Planning Guidance

38th Commandant of the Marine Corps

Priority Focus Areas:

- *Force Design*
- *Warfighting*
- *Education and Training*
- *Core Values*
- *Command and Leadership*

"I believe in my soul that Marines are different. Our identity is firmly rooted in our warrior ethos. This is the force that will always adapt and overcome no matter what the circumstances are. We fight and win in any clime and place."

— General David H. Berger

ORIENTATION AND INTENT

The *Commandant's Planning Guidance* (CPG) provides the 38th Commandant's strategic direction for the Marine Corps and mirrors the function of the Secretary of *Defense's Defense Planning Guidance* (DPG). It serves as the authoritative document for Service-level planning and provides a common direction to the Marine Corps Total Force. It also serves as a road map describing where the Marine Corps is going and why; what the Marine Corps force development priorities are and are not; and, in some instances, how and when prescribed actions will be implemented. This CPG serves as my Commandant's Intent for the next four years.

As Commandant Neller observed, "The Marine Corps is not organized, trained, equipped, or postured to meet the demands of the rapidly evolving future operating environment." I concur with his diagnosis. Significant change is required to ensure we are aligned with the 2018 *National Defense Strategy* (NDS) and DPG, and further, prepared to meet the demands of the Naval Fleet in executing current and emerging operational naval concepts. Effecting that change will be my top priority as your 38th Commandant.

This CPG outlines **my five priority focus areas: force design, warfighting, education and training, core values, and command and leadership**. I will use these focal areas as logical lines of effort to frame my thinking, planning, and decision-making at Headquarters Marine Corps (HQMC), as well as to communicate to our civilian leadership. This document explains how we will translate those focus areas into action with measurable outcomes. The institutional changes that follow this CPG will be based on a long-term view and singular focus on where we want the Marine Corps to be in the next 5-15 years, well beyond the tenure of any one Commandant, Presidential administration, or Congress. We cannot afford to retain outdated policies, doctrine, organizations, or force development strategies.

Unless specified within this document, all reference documents from previous Commandants are no longer authoritative; thus, Service and advocate-related publications using the *Marine Operating Concept or Force 2025* as "REF A" must be revised. Current advocate plans must be reviewed within the context of this guidance, and appropriate changes made. **We must communicate with precision and consistency, based on a common focus and a unified message**.

The coming decade will be characterized by conflict, crisis, and rapid change – just as every decade preceding it. And despite our best efforts, history demonstrates that we will fail to accurately predict every conflict; will be surprised by an unforeseen crisis; and may be late to fully grasp the implications of rapid change around us. The Arab Spring, West African Ebola Outbreak, Scarborough Shoal standoff, Russian invasion of eastern Ukraine, and weaponization of social media are but a few recent examples illustrating the point. While we must accept an environment characterized by uncertainty, we cannot ignore strong signals of change nor be complacent when it comes to designing and preparing the force for the future.

> *"We must communicate with precision and consistency, based on a common focus and a unified message."*

What is abundantly clear is that the future operating environment will place heavy demands on our Nation's Naval Services. Context and direction is clearly articulated in the NDS and DPG as well as testimony from our uniformed and civilian leadership. No further guidance is required; we are moving forward. **The Marine Corps will be trained and equipped as a naval expeditionary force-in-readiness and prepared to operate inside actively contested maritime spaces in support of fleet operations. In crisis prevention and crisis response, the Fleet Marine Force – acting as an extension of the Fleet – will be first on the scene, first to help, first to contain a brewing crisis, and first to fight if required to do so.** The Marine Corps will be the "force of choice" for the President, Secretary, and Combatant Commander – "a certain force for an uncertain world" as noted by Commandant Krulak. No matter what the crisis, our civilian leaders should always have one shared thought – *Send in the Marines.*

FORCE DESIGN

We should take pride in our force and recent operational successes, but the current force is not organized, trained, or equipped to support the naval force – operating in contested maritime spaces, facilitating sea control, or executing distributed maritime operations. We must change. We must divest of legacy capabilities that do not meet our future requirements, regardless of their past operational efficacy. There is no piece of equipment or major defense acquisition program that defines us – not the AAV, ACV, LAV, M1A1, M777, AH-1, F/A-18, F-35, or any other program. Likewise, we are not defined by any particular organizing construct – the Marine Air-Ground Task Force (MAGTF) cannot be our only solution for all crises. Instead, we are defined by our collective character as Marines and by fulfilling our Service roles and functions prescribed by Congress.

Force design is my number one priority. I have already initiated, and am personally leading, a future force design effort. Going forward, CD&I will be the only organization authorized to publish force development guidance on my behalf. We will divest of legacy defense programs and force structure that support legacy capabilities. **If provided the opportunity to secure additional modernization dollars in exchange for force structure, I am prepared to do so.** Plans or programs developed in support of this planning guidance that require additional resources must include an accompanying resource offset verified by a recognized analytic body (PA&E, OAD, etc.) to be considered for implementation.

NAVAL INTEGRATION

Adversary advances in long-range precision fires make closer naval integration an imperative. The focal point of the future integrated naval force will shift from traditional power projection to meet the new challenges associated with maintaining persistent naval forward presence to enable sea control and denial operations. The Fleet Marine Force (FMF) will support the Joint Force Maritime Component Command (JFMCC) and fleet commander concept of operations, especially in close and confined seas, where enemy long-range precision fires threaten maneuver by traditional large-signature naval platforms. Future naval force development and employment will include new capabilities that will ensure that the Navy-Marine Corps team cannot be excluded from any region in advancing or protecting our national interests or those of our allies. Marines will focus on exploiting positional advantage and defending key maritime terrain that enables persistent sea control and denial operations forward. Together, the Navy-Marine Corps Team will enable the joint force to partner, persist and operate forward despite adversary employment of long-range precision fires.

In addition to the recent focus on operational integration, I intend to seek greater integration between the Navy and Marine Corps in our Program Objective Memorandum (POM) development process. We share a common understanding of the NDS, the pacing threat, the future operating environment, and of those capabilities that provide the greatest overmatch for our Navy. We must strive to create capabilities that support fleet operations and naval campaigns. We will integrate our POM wargaming efforts with the Navy's, thereby, ensuring a common understanding and common baseline from which each Service can communicate their needs to the Secretary of the Navy, and ultimately, the Secretary of Defense.

Fleet Marine Force and Navy-Marine Corps Component Command Relationship

In 1933, the establishment of the FMF under the operational control of the Fleet Commander generated great unity of effort, operational flexibility, and the integrated application of Navy and Marine capabilities throughout the maritime domain. The 1986 Goldwater-Nichols Act, however, removed the preponderance of the FMF from fleet operational control and disrupted the long-standing Navy-Marine Corps relationship by creating separate Navy and Marine Corps components within joint forces. Furthermore, Navy and Marine Corps officers developed a tendency to view their operational responsibilities as separate and distinct, rather than intertwined. With the rise of both land and sea-based threats to the global commons, there is a need to re-establish a more integrated approach to operations in the maritime domain. Reinvigorating the FMF can be accomplished by assigning more Marine Corps forces to the Fleet, putting Marine Corps experts in the fleet Maritime Operations Centers, and also by shifting emphasis in our training, education, and supporting establishment activities. Refining the component relationship, within the framework of Goldwater-Nichols, is a more complicated issue that must be explored in partnership with the Navy. With one exception, our MARFORs are not operational headquarters, nor will they be resourced as such. Our MARFORs are intended as administrative headquarters that advise their respective commands on the Marine Corps. In a functional component construct, we will complement and augment the JFMCC.

Marine Expeditionary Forces

The Marine Expeditionary Force (MEF) will remain our principal warfighting organization; however, our MEFs need not be identical. III MEF will become our main focus-of-effort, designed to provide U.S. Indo-Pacific Command (U.S. INDOPACOM) and the Commander, 7th Fleet with a fight-tonight, stand-in force capability to persist inside an adversary's weapon systems threat range, create a mutually contested space, and facilitate the larger naval campaign. When modernized in a manner consistent with the vision above, III MEF will be a credible deterrent to adversary aggression in the Pacific. I MEF will also be focused on supporting the Commander, USINDOPACOM and the Commander, 3rd Fleet. I MEF will continue to provide forces to USINDOPACOM to build partner capacity and reinforce deterrence efforts, and must be prepared to impose costs on a potential adversary, globally. We will increasingly accept risk with I MEF's habitual relationship with CENTCOM; however, 7th Marines is at present purpose-built to support CENTCOM requirements; thus, I MEF will continue to support CENTCOM requirements within the capacity of 7th Marines. II MEF will undergo substantial changes to better align with the needs of Commanders of 2d and 6th Fleets. During a major contingency operation or sustained campaign ashore, necessary combat power will be provided to the committed MEF through global sourcing by the Total Force.

We will continue to recommend Marine operating forces be employed as combined-arms teams; however, we must be flexible enough to satisfy Fleet and Combatant Commander needs whether they require a MEF, a single LHA with Marine complement in support of an Expeditionary Strike Group (ESG), or an aviation detachment in support of U.S. Special Operations Command (USSOCOM). First and foremost, we must be prepared to be employed as Fleet Marine Forces. The Service will provide ready forces, and our component headquarters will advise their respective commanders on the best employment of those forces; however, the ultimate decision on tactical employment resides with the Combatant Commanders.

Marine Expeditionary Units and Forward Deployed Forces

As Commandant Krulak noted nearly 25 years ago, the Marine Expeditionary Unit (MEU) "is the jewel in our crown, and must be kept ready, relevant, and capable." Regrettably, it no longer has the same relevance as it once had to the Fleet; however, this will change. We will consider employment models of the Amphibious Ready Group (ARG) / MEU other than the traditional three-ship model. We will accept and prepare for Fleet Commander employment of LHA/Ds as part of three-ship ESGs as desired. I see potential in the "Lightning Carrier" concept, based on an LHA / LHD; however, do not support a new-build CVL. Partnering a big-deck amphib with surface combatants is the right warfighting capability for many of the challenges confronting the joint force, and provides substantial naval and Joint operational flexibility, lethality, and survivability.

The majority of defense professionals continue to support our conclusions regarding the efficacy of forward deployed forces even if they question the affordability of such forces. I will continue to advocate for the continued forward deployment of our forces globally to compete against the malign activities of China, Russia, Iran, and their proxies – with a prioritized focus on China's One Belt One Road initiative and Chinese malign activities in the East and South China Seas. This is not intended to be a defense of the status quo as our forces currently forward deployed lack the requisite capabilities to deter our adversaries and persist in a contested space to facilitate sea denial. While I will continue to support and advocate for the Unit Deployment Program, we must revise the program to ensure those forces and capabilities deployed to the Western Pacific create a competitive advantage and facilitate deterrence in the INDOPACOM Theater. One possible future would be the forward deployment of multiple High-Mobility Artillery Rocket System (HIMARS) batteries armed with long-range anti-ship missiles.

In addition to deterring aggression and supporting naval operations, our forward deployed forces will remain ready to respond to crises globally as the force-in-readiness. While we will retain the capability to deploy as organic combined-arms teams or as part of a Joint Task Force (JTF), Marines aboard L-Class ships as part of an ARG or ESG will remain the benchmark for our forward operating crisis response forces. We must increase the lethality of the ARG, and must accept new employment models that will increase the relevance of

ARG to the Fleet Commanders. There is no one-size fits-all solution to the operational challenges confronting the Fleets; thus, we should be willing to accept more than one tailored solution to ARG organization and employment. We must preserve those elements of our current organization that remain relevant and jettison those that do not. What served us well yesterday may not today, and may not in the future. We must continually seek improvements with an eye toward the future – specifically changes in technology – and consider what adaptations we need to make.

Naval Force Development

During World War II, we as a Service, clearly understood that Marines operated in support of the Navy's sea control mission. In subsequent years, the luxury of presumptive maritime superiority deluded us into thinking the Navy existed to support "Marine" operations ashore. That era was an historic anomaly, and **we need to re-focus on how we will fulfill our mandate to support the Fleet**. That starts by educating ourselves on the operational challenges to sea control, especially in terms of capability and capacity issues, and then discussing with our Navy partners the best path to achieve the desired outcomes.

While the answer to the question "What does the Navy provide the Marine Corps?" is readily identifiable – operational and strategic mobility and assured access – the same cannot be said for the follow-on question, "What does the Marine Corps provide the Navy and the Joint Force?" Traditionally, the answer has been power projection forces from the sea and/or forces for sustained operations ashore in support of a traditional naval campaign. We should ask ourselves – what do the Fleet Commanders want from the Marine Corps, and what does the Navy need from the Marine Corps?

Future Amphibious Capability and Force Development

Our Nation's ability to project power and influence beyond its shores is increasingly challenged by long-range precision fires; expanding air, surface, and sub-surface threats; and the continued degradation of our amphibious and auxiliary ship readiness. The ability to project and maneuver from strategic distances will likely be detected and contested from the point of embarkation during a major contingency. Our naval expeditionary forces must possess a variety of deployment options, including L-class and E-class ships, but also increasingly look to other available options such as unmanned platforms, stern landing vessels,

other ocean-going connectors, and smaller more lethal and more risk-worthy platforms. **We must continue to seek the affordable and plentiful at the expense of the exquisite and few when conceiving of the future amphibious portion of the fleet.**

We must also explore new options, such as inter-theater connectors and commercially available ships and craft that are smaller and less expensive, thereby increasing the affordability and allowing acquisition at a greater quantity. We recognize that we must distribute our forces ashore given the growth of adversary precision strike capabilities, so it would be illogical to continue to concentrate our forces on a few large ships. The adversary will quickly recognize that striking while concentrated (aboard ship) is the preferred option. We need to change this calculus with a new fleet design of smaller, more lethal, and more risk-worthy platforms. We must be fully integrated with the Navy to develop a vision and a new fleet architecture that can be successful against our peer adversaries while also maintaining affordability. To achieve this difficult task, the Navy and Marine Corps must ensure larger surface combatants possess mission agility across sea control, littoral, and amphibious operations, while we concurrently expand the quantity of more specialized manned and unmanned platforms.

As the preeminent littoral warfare and expeditionary warfare service, we must engage in a more robust discussion regarding naval expeditionary forces and capabilities not currently resident within the Marine Corps such as coastal / riverine forces, naval construction forces, and mine countermeasure forces. We must ask ourselves whether it is prudent to absorb some of those functions, forces, and capabilities to create a single naval expeditionary force whereby the Commandant could better ensure their readiness and resourcing.

Power Projection and Force Development

We will no longer use a "2.0 MEB requirement" as the foundation for our arguments regarding amphibious ship building, to determine the requisite capacity of vehicles or other capabilities, or as pertains to the Maritime Prepositioning Force. We will no longer reference the 38-ship requirement memo from 2009, or the 2016 Force Structure Assessment, as the basis for our arguments and force structure justifications. The ongoing 2019 Force Structure Assessment will inform the amphibious requirements based upon this guidance. The global options for amphibs include many more options than simply LHAs, LPDs, and LSDs. I will work closely with the Secretary of the Navy and Chief of Naval Operations (CNO) to ensure there are adequate numbers of the right types of ships, with the right capabilities, to meet national requirements.

I do not believe joint forcible entry operations (JFEO) are irrelevant or an operational anachronism; however, we must acknowledge that different approaches are required given the proliferation of anti-access/area denial (A2AD) threat capabilities in mutually contested spaces. Visions of a massed naval armada nine nautical miles off-shore in the South China Sea preparing to launch the landing force in swarms of ACVs, LCUs, and LCACs are impractical and unreasonable. We must accept the realities created by the proliferation of precision long-range fires, mines, and other smart-weapons, and seek innovative ways to overcome those threat capabilities. I encourage experimentation with lethal long-range unmanned systems capable of traveling 200 nautical miles, penetrating into the adversary enemy threat ring, and crossing the shoreline – causing the adversary to allocate resources to eliminate the threat, create dilemmas, and further create opportunities for fleet maneuver. We cannot wait to identify solutions to our mine countermeasure needs, and must make this a priority for our future force development efforts.

Although our future force will be applied to problems and conflicts globally, we cannot afford to build multiple forces optimized for a specific competency such as arctic warfare, urban operations, or desert warfare. We will build one force – optimized for naval expeditionary warfare in contested spaces, purpose-built to facilitate sea denial and assured access in support of the fleets. That single purpose-built future force will be applied against other challenges across the globe; however, we will not seek to hedge or balance our investments to account for those contingencies.

Force Development Tasks and Responsibilities

In recent years, Service Chiefs have publicly called for streamlined force development and acquisition processes, and Congress has taken steps toward improvement. Over the past several decades, the laws, policies, and practices associated with this topic have changed significantly, but Marine Corps orders and directives have not kept pace. We will generate a comprehensive, yet succinct and understandable, hierarchy of orders and directives that define roles and responsibilities within the enterprise, with a particular emphasis on what, when, and how transitions between activities are conducted and how progress toward

established goals is monitored. These documents will be crafted as "mission-type orders" that define the tasks, and their respective purposes, performed by the Deputy Commandants, rather than detailed instructions that bog down in process minutiae. Each Deputy Commandant will similarly produce orders that define their subordinate units' tasks. To be clear, the Deputy Commandant for Combat Development and Integration has primary responsibility for all Marine Corps force development, with all other Deputy Commandants in support as "advocates" who can provide subject matter expertise in their respective fields, rather than as "advocates" who direct force development action.

Maritime Prepositioning Force

For several decades, the Maritime Prepositioning Force (MPF) represented a competitive advantage for the Marine Corps. That is less the case today. During a major contingency, our MPF ships would be highly vulnerable and difficult to protect. We must be prepared to fundamentally alter this capability, as well as all the inventory currently programmed for inclusion with the MPF, as we rethink the future of this capability.

Joint Task Force (JTF) Headquarters and Joint Operations

Our force must be an integral element of the Joint Force, able to combine people, processes, and programs to execute globally integrated operations. Historically, we focused joint integration efforts at headquarters and command elements, as opposed to integrating capabilities at the individual unit-level. Moving forward, the Marine Corps must maximize our inherent relationship with the Navy, along with our expertise coordinating elements of the MAGTF, to effectively coordinate across all warfighting domains to support the Joint Force. Our Service concepts and doctrine must provide relevant joint capabilities; we must be able to communicate and collaborate across interoperable systems and equipment; and our professional military education (PME) and training programs must enable Marines to gain and maintain an understanding of joint operations, thereby preparing our leaders to fully maximize joint and coalition warfare. Joint operations are a warfighting advantage and the Marine Corps must fully embrace our role as a critical enabler to the Joint Force.

Reserve Component Forces

While organized and equipped congruently, we cannot expect our Selected Marine Corps Reserve (SMCR) units to maintain the same levels of readiness as our Active Component units. What we desire and expect in our SMCR units and Individual Ready Reserve (IRR) are Marines and units "ready for mobilization." Once mobilized, our Reserve Component forces will undergo additional pre-deployment training to achieve the necessary readiness for deployment and employment.

We will examine the merits of formalizing command relationships between Active and Reserve Component units. Just as our Active Component will change, so will our Reserve Component. As part of our force design effort, we will explore the efficacy of fully integrating our reserve units within the Active Component, as well as other organizational options.

Installations & Infrastructure

While experts across the force developed an Infrastructure and Reset Plan, we have collectively failed to aggressively execute it; thus, creating a cascading effect of negative second and third order effects. Our installation infrastructure is untenable. We are encumbered by 19,000 buildings, some of which are beyond the scope of repair and should instead be considered for demolition. These excess structures spread limited facilities, sustainment, restoration, and modernization (FSRM) resources thinly across the enterprise, impeding our ability to focus efforts and achieve desired outcomes. We have under-funded maintenance at our installations for far too long and failed to appreciate the growing risks associated with those decisions. Moreover, our training facilities and ranges are antiquated, and the force lacks the necessary modern simulators to sustain training readiness. To make matters worse, we created separate chains of command for our installations and the operating forces they support, further inducing friction and inefficiency. Modernizing our force structure requires a deliberate review of our installations and a deliberate plan to invest, divest, and reset.

Executive Decision Making

I intend be an active participant in decision-making within HQMC, but I do not expect to make all decisions, nor do I believe that all decisions require Marine Requirements Oversight Council (MROC) review. I expect Deputy Commandants to make service-level decisions in accordance with this guidance. Further, while current decision-making bodies like the MROC can be effective forums, they must adapt to the accelerating pace of change or risk being marginalized or eliminated. Our

processes should be inclusive, but we cannot allow a desire for consensus to stifle initiative or result in staff paralysis. We will review the efficacy of the MROC Review Board (MRB) and MROC to make appropriate changes.

Every activity within HQMC must support the POM build and inform the planning, programming, budgeting, and execution (PPBE) process. Our current structures and processes fail to meet this standard. Advocates help prioritize and recommend force development based on the positions and capabilities identified by the Operating Forces (OPFOR) but they do not decide. Advocacy supports force development, and thus should occur within and emanate from CD&I. As part of our revised force development and POM processes, we require two outcomes: integration with the Navy and an independently verifiable analytic foundation to our program. We currently lack both. The current advocacy order will be replaced.

PEOPLE

Everything starts and ends with the individual Marine. The principal challenge facing the Marine Corps today lies in continuing to fulfill its charter as the naval expeditionary force-in-readiness, while simultaneously modernizing the force in accordance with the NDS, doing both with a leaner force structure, potentially fewer Marines, and a possible reduction in total resources. Marines are the centerpiece of the Corps – our principal emphasis must focus on recruiting; educating and training; instilling our core values and sense of accountability; equipping; and treating them with dignity, care, and concern.

Taking Care of Marines

"Taking care of Marines" includes holding Marines to high professional standards of performance, conduct, and discipline. Leaders are expected to do everything within their power to ensure the individual Marine succeeds, but there are limits to our abilities to sustain the transformation of the individuals who simply choose to opt out. Marines failing to adhere to our standards or failing to remain competitive within their occupational fields or grade will be separated. Demanding superior performance and enforcing high standards should not be viewed as draconian, but rather, should be expected by professionals. We will not accept mediocrity within the force and, above all, must seek to remove those from within our ranks who are adversely impacting the overall readiness of our force. We must seek the administrative separation of those unable to be promoted who are creating an artificial barrier for advancement of more motivated individuals; we must seek the separation of those unable to deploy or assist in the training and education of Marines preparing for deployment; and must energetically seek the removal of all individuals engaged in destructive behaviors such as hazing. I will communicate additional guidance to all commanders in the near future establishing guidelines and my expectations.

Parental Leave / Maternity Leave

We should never ask our Marines to choose between being the best parent possible and the best Marine possible. These outcomes should never be in competition to the extent that success with one will come at the expense of the other. Our parental / maternity leave policies are inadequate and have failed to keep pace with societal norms and modern talent management practices. We fully support the growth of our Marine families, and will do everything possible to provide parents with opportunities to remain with their newborns for extended periods of time. In the future, we will consider up to one year leaves-of-absence for mothers to remain with their children before returning to full duty to complete their service obligations.

Manpower

Our manpower system was designed in the industrial era to produce mass, not quality. We assumed that quantity of personnel was the most important element of the system, and that workers (Marines) are all essentially interchangeable. As the complexity of the world has increased, the spread between physical jobs and thinking jobs has increased dramatically. War still has a physical component, and all Marines need to be screened and ready to fight. However, we have not adapted to the needs of the current battlefield. The only way to attract and retain Marines capable of winning on the new battlefield is to compete with the tools and incentives available to them in the marketplace.

Talent Management

The essence of all manpower systems is to encourage those you need and want to stay, and separate who are not performing to standards. Our current system lacks the authorities and tools to accomplish that simple outcome in anything but a blunt way. Our manpower model is based primarily on time and experience, not talent or performance or potential future performance.

While performance is factored into promotion selection, it is narrowed to a slim cohort, roughly based on year groups – an antiquated model. Additionally, the Service does not have the tools needed to recruit the skills it wants, retain specific talents, advance Marines more quickly based on need, and separate Marines who cannot perform or are not compatible with military service. These deficiencies are related to budget, policy, and law.

The current manpower model does not accommodate a Marine whose interests change over time, tends to average performance over time instead of weighting current performance more heavily, forces Marines to move out of skills they excel at in the name of developing them, and cuts careers off near the 20-year mark when workers have decades of productivity left in them. These polices drive increased PCS costs, throw away talent at the point it is most productive and highly trained, and discourage performers who would like to continue serving, but may be less interested in promotion or constant disruptive moves of questionable personal and professional value.

In the current manpower model, primary occupational fields are set early in a career and Marines are essentially stuck either accepting it for an entire career or choosing separation. Even talented, high-performing officers have changing interests over time. Additionally, the lack of incentives for self-improvement through education and personnel development discourages those inclined to learn, think, and innovate – as these tend to disrupt the current model, and may in fact make the individual less competitive for promotion.

An incentives-based model would offer the ability to target incentives to specific individuals the Service wants to retain. We should use money like a focused weapon, and aim it at the exact individual we need. Currently, we target people via a mass fires approach, instead of more selective targeting. While we hope this results in the retention of the most talented, our antiquated models may also retain poor performers. The options for a new model are numerous. One could easily envision a model with a higher percentage of below zone promotions on every board; thus, facilitating the advancement of more talented and less costly Marines. Early retirements may induce lower performers out at the lowest long-term encumbrance, while incentivizing high performers to stay. Inducing low performers out accelerates the opportunities of all those who remain in the system; thus, further ensuring the most talented force possible.

In order to improve our current manpower model, we must take steps to increase standards at every rank, recruit more talented individuals, use every authority currently available, trim end-strength in favor of quality, and request Congress for more modern tools to compete in today's economy. Modest improvement can be achieved with the tools already in hand, while dramatic improvement will likely take changes in budgets, law (DOPMA), policy, traditions, and mindset. I will communicate more on this idea in the near future.

Fitness Reports

Despite a major reform effort in 1996, there are major shortcomings in our current Performance Evaluation System that must be addressed. As was true then, there is a growing lack of faith within our ranks in the system's ability to accurately identify their skills, performance, and future potential. Upward growth and mobility must favor the most talented within our ranks while facilitating the identification of those with a special aptitude as instructors, educators, commanders, staff officers, mentors, or with special technical skills. We must and will remedy these shortfalls.

As we investigate potential modifications to the current system and reports, we should evaluate the merits of the following changes at a minimum:

- Provide the Marine Reported On (MRO) with an opportunity at self-assessment

- Modify the report in a manner that allows the reporting senior (RS) and reporting officer (RO) to identify future potential

- Modify the report in a manner that allows the RS and RO to identify individuals with special aptitudes for training, educating, mentoring, technical skills, planning, etc.

- Weight the reports so that a three-month report is not valued in a congruent manner to a 12 month report.

- Weight command over non-command reports, and combat over non-combat reports.

- Eliminate academic fitness reports as non-observed reports. The goal of the academic report should be to accurately identify the individual's success while in school and then determine future potential in the next rank/grade or as an instructor.

- Weight academic reports in a manner that rewards the individual Marine for resident PME and their performance in that setting.

- Identify the cumulative performance of the RS and RO; thus, ensuring that Marines with poor relative values themselves aren't adversely impacting the careers of more talented individuals they complete reports on.

While we will continue to maintain a total force approach to force development to include training and education, we must accept the realities related to periods of annual training completed by our Reserve Component (RC) Marines. For many, these periods of service require an Active Component Marine to complete a fitness report covering two weeks. Because these reports are weighted the same as every other report within a RS's profile, they are habitually a low relative value to avoid artificially skewing the RS's profile. While this is understandable, it should not endure. We must provide the RS with an opportunity to evaluate the individual's performance in relation to every other RC Marine the RS has evaluated completing similar training, and not attempt to judge the two week performance against periods usually covering six months – if not longer.

WARFIGHTING

As good as we are today, we will need to be even better tomorrow to maintain our warfighting overmatch. We will achieve this through the strength of our innovation, ingenuity, and willingness to continually adapt to and initiate changes in the operating environment to affect the behavior of real-world pacing threats. This will require a break from the past practice of capability-based force development. We will succeed by continually challenging the status quo and asking ourselves – is there a way to cause a better outcome? Will III MEF be able to create a mutually contested space in the South or East China Seas if directed to do so by U.S. INDOPACOM? If not, what changes are required to enable the desired outcomes? Will we create the modern, lethal naval expeditionary force we seek by continuing to maintain separate and distinct capability development and POM development processes from the Navy? If not, is there a better way to cause the desired outcomes?

The Marine Corps has been and remains the Nation's premier naval expeditionary force-in-readiness. While we stand by to perform "such other duties as the President may direct," foreign humanitarian assistance, disaster relief, and noncombatant evacuations do not define us – they are not our identity. Rather, they are the day-to-day consequence of being the force-in-readiness. As the force-in-readiness, we are not an across-the-ROMO force; but rather, a force that ensures the prevention of major conflict and deters the escalation of conflict within the ROMO.

Command and Control

We must reach and execute effective military decisions faster than our adversaries in any conflict setting, on any scale. Our command and control processes and systems must reflect our maneuver warfare philosophy. Decision making that focuses on speed and creating tempo, mission command that focuses on low level initiative, simple planning processes and orders writing techniques that are measured by the quality of the intent, all require a command and control system that is flexible, adaptable, and resilient. We will always focus on people over systems in the command and control process per FMFM1. Decisions are what the commander does; systems exist only to support the commander's needs. We must also recognize that modern operations, particularly distributed operations, require connectivity and access for success. We must create systems that are resilient and match our warfighting approach in order to protect our ability to make decisions that generate tempo.

WARFIGHTING CONCEPTS AND FORCE DEVELOPMENT

Naval Operating Concepts

As a naval service, the Marine Corps contributes substantively in the development of the naval operational concepts that will guide how the joint force conducts expeditionary operations in the future. The character of war is increasingly dynamic, and the rapid advance of new technologies by both friend and foe has accelerated the rate of change, ensuring that the character of war in the future will be much different than that of the recent past. Our most challenging adversaries have initiated a new paradigm of warfare, based on the development and fielding of long-range precision weapons, as well as information-related capabilities. The greatly extended range, quantity, and accuracy of these observed fires impose new vulnerabilities on the joint force, to include the Navy and Marine Corps, and necessitate significant changes to the concepts and capabilities by which Marines will conduct expeditionary operations in the immediate future.

The 2016 *Marine Corps Operating Concept* (MOC) predates the current set of national strategy and guidance documents, but it was prescient in many ways. It directed partnering with the Navy to develop two concepts, *Littoral Operations in a Contested Environment* (LOCE) and *Expeditionary Advanced Base Operations* (EABO) that nest exceptionally well with the current strategic guidance. It is time to move beyond the MOC itself, however, and partner with the Navy to complement LOCE and EABO with classified, threat-specific operating concepts that describe how naval forces will conduct the range of missions articulated in our strategic guidance. The MOC will therefore be replaced by either a Marine Corps or unified capstone naval concept as determined in consultation with the Chief of Naval Operations. With respect to subordinate concepts, at a minimum I see the need for a concept that describes how naval forces compete and, if necessary, confront adversaries below the threshold of conflict, as well as a concept for how we will conduct sea-based forward presence and crisis response.

Composite Warfare

As an organization statutorily designated for service with the Fleet during the prosecution of a naval campaign, the Marine Corps must be able to quickly and effectively integrate into the naval force. The Navy's method for decentralized command and control at the tactical-level is composite warfare (CW); therefore, the Marine Corps must prepare to operate within this doctrinal construct. CW provides flexible command and control arrangements that can respond to multiple threats across various domains and mission areas without overwhelming the decision capacity of a single commander or battle staff. Through this approach to all-domain warfare, CW empowers subordinates to execute decentralized tactical operations – independently or integrated into a larger Naval or Joint Force – through mission command and flexible supporting relationships responsive to ever-changing tactical situations.

Marine Corps integration into the Fleet via composite warfare will be a prerequisite to the successful execution of amphibious operations: Marines cannot be passive passengers en route to the amphibious objective area. As long-range precision stand-off weapons improve and diffuse along the world's littorals, Marines must contribute to the fight alongside our Navy shipmates from the moment we embark. Once ashore, Marine Forces operating within CW will increase the Fleet's lethality and resiliency and will contribute to all domain access, deterrence, sea control, and power projection.

The Marine Corps will add composite warfare to our practical application of naval tactical combat power to complement our understanding of maneuver warfare outlined in FMFM-1 *Warfighting*. The Marine Corps will undergo an aggressive naval education program – ranging from the conceptual understanding naval theory and history down to tactical-level schools and courses – to enable our commanders and staffs across the Fleet Marine Force to quickly integrate in to naval forces and provide critical capabilities both afloat and ashore. Conversely, the Marine Corps must advance the education of navy officers in our capabilities and organizations; without this reciprocity, our efforts will not be as effective as the future security environment requires. We will conduct a comprehensive review of all doctrinal, reference, and warfighting publications to ensure that our doctrine, concepts, tactics, and procedures nest within and support composite warfare; modification will be necessary with those that do not. We will assess our current staffs for their ability to integrate in to composite warfare, modifying them where appropriate to increase naval force lethality. Last, we will provide personnel to navy staffs ranging from numbered Fleets through type squadrons in order to create standing naval staffs capable of fighting both Navy and Marine forces immediately.

Stand-In Forces

Over the coming months, we will release a new concept in support of the Navy's *Distributed Maritime Operations* (DMO) Concept and the NDS called – *Stand-in Forces*. The *Stand-in Forces* concept is designed to restore the strategic initiative to naval forces and empower our allies and partners to successfully confront regional hegemons that infringe on their territorial boundaries and interests. **Stand-in Forces are designed to generate technically disruptive, tactical stand-in engagements that confront aggressor naval forces with an array of low signature, affordable, and risk-worthy platforms and payloads.** Stand-in forces take advantage of the relative strength of the contemporary defense and rapidly-emerging new technologies to create an integrated maritime defense that is optimized to operate in close and confined seas in defiance of adversary long-range precision "stand-off capabilities."

Creating new capabilities that intentionally initiate stand-in engagements is a disruptive "button hook" in force development that runs counter to the action that our adversaries anticipate. Rather than heavily investing in expensive and exquisite capabilities that regional aggressors have optimized their forces to target, naval forces will persist forward with many smaller, low signature, affordable platforms that can economically host a dense array of lethal and non-lethal payloads.

By exploiting the technical revolution in autonomy, advanced manufacturing, and artificial intelligence, the naval forces can create many new risk-worthy unmanned and minimally-manned platforms that can be employed in stand-in engagements to create tactical dilemmas that adversaries will confront when attacking our allies and forces forward. Stand-in Forces will be supported from expeditionary advanced bases (EABs) and will complement the low signature of the EABs with an equally low signature force structure comprised largely of unmanned platforms that operate ashore, afloat, submerged, and aloft in close concert to overwhelm enemy platforms.

Stand-in Forces take advantage of the strategic offensive and tactical defense to create disproportionate result at affordable cost. Because they are inherently resilient, risk worthy, inexpensive and lethal they restore combat credibility to forward deployed naval forces and serve to deter aggression. Stand-in force capabilities are much better optimized to confront physical aggression and malign behaviors with physical presence and non-lethal payloads, empowering allies with the ability to defend their own national territory and interests

Expeditionary Advanced Based Operations (EABO)

EABO complement the Navy's *Distributed Maritime Operations* Concept and will inform how we approach missions against peer adversaries. As we move beyond concept to implementation, we must recognize that EABO is not a "thing" – it is a category of operations. Saying we will *do* EABO is akin to saying we will *do* amphibious operations, and as with amphibious operations, EABO can take many forms.

EABO are driven by the aforementioned adversary deployment of long-range precision fires designed to support a strategy of "counter-intervention" directed against U.S. and coalition forces. EABO, as an operational concept, enables the naval force to persist forward within the arc of adversary long-range precision fires to support our treaty partners with combat credible forces on a much more resilient and difficult to target forward basing infrastructure. EABO are designed to restore force resiliency and enable the persistent naval forward presence that has long been the hallmark of naval forces. Most significantly, EABO reverse the cost imposition that determined adversaries seek to impose on the joint force. EABO guide an apt and appropriate adjustment in future naval force development to obviate the significant investment our adversaries have made in long-range precision fires. Potential adversaries intend to target our forward fixed and vulnerable bases, as well as deep water ports, long runways, large signature platforms, and ships. By developing a new expeditionary naval force structure that is not dependent on concentrated, vulnerable, and expensive forward infrastructure and platforms, we will frustrate enemy efforts to separate U.S. Forces from our allies and interests. EABO enable naval forces to partner and persist forward to control and deny contested areas where legacy naval forces cannot be prudently employed without accepting disproportionate risk.

EABO enable the U.S. Navy and Marine Corps to partner and persist forward despite adversary long-range precision fires, a necessary reaction to adversary force development initiatives. However, our ambitions are more aggressive than preserving status quo options, and we seek to restore the strategic initiative by establishing a disruptive and highly competitive space where American ingenuity can capitalize on the new capabilities that naval forces will exploit to deter conflict and dominate confined seas. The U.S. Navy and Marine Corps do not seek to merely "discern the future operating environment," but are determined to define the future character of maritime conflict, so that naval forces will deter or fight from a position of enduring advantage. Inevitably, EABO will evolve in implementation into a wide array of missions, with an equally wide assortment of force and capability combinations required to support them.

Success will be defined in terms of finding the smallest, lowest signature options that yield the maximum operational utility. We must always be mindful of the ratio of operational contribution to employment cost. We will test various forms of EABO against specific threats and ask ourselves whether EABO contributions to the joint force are worth its logistics and security burden. This ratio should always be more favorable than other joint force options contributing a similar capability.

To date, our wargaming has focused on a limited set of scenarios; thus, we will need to expand our analysis across more scenarios to better inform our force design efforts. As in earlier design initiatives, such as seabasing, we are going to build a force that can do EABO opposed to building an EABO force. This distinction is important because our fundamental design principles are independent of EABO. A force composed of highly capable tactical units that can perform combined arms operations at all echelons, enabled by organic air and logistics is a force that can perform EABO – if provided tailored capabilities and training. Determining the exact nature of this specialized training and equipping will be the focus of our EAB implementation actions.

Distributed Operations

New threats, new missions, and new technologies require us to adjust our organizational design and modernize our capabilities. While others may wait for a clearer picture of the future operating environment, we will focus our efforts on driving change and influencing future operating environment outcomes. One way to drive the continued evolution of the future operating environment is Distributed Operations (DO). DO capable forces are a critically important component of Marine Corps modernization.

Traditionally, the infantry company has been the lowest echelon capable of coordinating the full-range of combined arms, but miniaturization of electronics and increased processing power enable adversaries to empower individuals and small units with combined-arms capability. We must be equal or better than this threat by pushing combined arms to the squad.

Given the imperative for a new force design, codifying DO is critical to implementation. We have been experimenting with DO for two decades, but it is still inadequately developed and lacks a doctrinal foundation, thus it has not driven unit or organizational design, nor has it adequately informed our investment decisions. We will refine DO through experimentation and force-on-force training and by summer 2020, we will begin writing it into doctrine. Our findings will also guide our concurrent Force Design activities.

Our lack of progress in implementing DO is in part due to an inadequate description of why we would distribute forces and why we would conduct distributed operations. In my judgment, we distribute for five reasons:

- We disperse to better accomplish the mission against a distant or distributed adversary.

- We disperse to improve maneuver options in order to gain a positional advantage to assault, or engage more effectively with direct or indirect fires.

- We disperse to reduce the effects of enemy fires.

- We disperse to impose costs and induce uncertainty.

- We disperse to reduce our signature to avoid detection. In a precision strike regime, sensing first and shooting first are a tremendous advantage.

We will structure our experimentation and training to capture the benefits of DO and begin codifying it into doctrine.

Future Force Development

Future force development requires a wider range of force options and capabilities. The Marine Corps must be able to fight at sea, from the sea, and from the land to the sea; operate and persist within range of adversary long-range fires; maneuver across the seaward and landward portions of complex littorals; and sense, shoot, and sustain while combining the physical and information domains to achieve desired outcomes. Achieving this endstate requires a force that can create the virtues of mass without the vulnerabilities of concentration, thanks to mobile and low-signature sensors and weapons. Our desired endstate also requires elite warriors with physical and mental toughness, tenacity, initiative, and aggressiveness to innovate, adapt, and win in a rapidly-changing operating environment.

The amphibious fleet and littoral maneuver craft also require significant future force development. The amphibious fleet must be diversified in composition and increased in capacity by developing smaller, specialized ships, as a complement to the existing family of large multipurpose ships. Doing so will improve resilience, dispersion, and the ability to operate in complex archipelagoes and contested littorals without incurring unacceptable risk. Initial options for examination include:

- A "hybrid" amphibious ship to transport landing craft and enable the ability to fight in a contested littoral.

- An inexpensive, self-deploying "connector" capable of delivering rolling stock on or near-shore in a contested littoral.

- Considering how a wider array of smaller "black bottom" ships might supplement the maritime preposition and amphibious fleets.

Future force development must also contribute to an integrated operational architecture and enable information environment operations. Friendly forces must be able to disguise actions and intentions, as well as deceive the enemy, through the use of decoys, signature management, and signature reduction. **Preserving the ability to command and control in a contested information network environment is paramount.**

Last, we must prioritize research, development, and fielding of emerging and advanced technologies that are applicable within the seaward and landward portions of the littorals. Technologies such as artificial intelligence, robotics, additive manufacturing, quantum computing, and nanotechnology will continue to change the world - we must be positioned to capture the returns on investment. Similarly, unmanned and autonomous systems will enable greater applications for hydrographic survey, reconnaissance, mine warfare, logistics support, deception, and warfighting. Nascent applications such as swarming and miniature aerial attack systems have the potential to radically change the character of war. Our future force development must include appropriate prioritization in these technologies; however, doing so will not be easy. It will require divesting of legacy capabilities that cannot be economically adapted to meet the demands of the future, while also taking calculated risks in some areas.

WARFIGHTING INVESTMENTS AND DIVESTMENTS

Talent retention

Retention of the most talented individuals within the institution is critical. In order to realize the F-35 capability, cyber capability, AI / Data Science capability, Group 5 UAS and UGV capability, or DO / EABO capability articulated in our concepts, we must reverse the negative trends related to talent retention. This is not a Marine Corps problem; but rather, a joint force problem. This will likely require policy changes as well as adjustments to retention bonuses. If we desire the force articulated in our concepts, then talent retention must be a priority. Just as we will focus on precision fires, our talent management and talent retention efforts must be executed with precision. The blanket provision of bonuses across entire communities will no longer be our weapon-of-choice; but rather, we will seek a more precise option to ensure the most talented individuals – to include those identified as the most competent and capable combat leaders and not just those with the most expensive technical training.

Training and Education

We must change the Training and Education Continuum from an industrial age model, to an information age model. To that end, we need to determine the best way to effect the desired change, which includes the way we select, train and evaluate instructors throughout the continuum, but also the way we inspect formal school houses. At present, our entire system for formal schools management reinforces the industrial age model and therefore needs to be changed. But first, we must codify what is meant by an information age model of training and educating Marines. We have some of this going

on across the continuum, but it needs to be the norm, not the exception. We will prioritize funding in support of this transformation.

In addition, we will prioritize funding aimed at further reinforcing the transformation. We must continue to strengthen the process whereby we reinforce the transformation that occurs at Officer Candidate School (OCS) and Recruit Training. This means continuously optimizing MOS production management to limit Marines awaiting training as much as possible, as well as ensuring that while they are waiting, there is a plan for using their time as constructively as possible – to include additional educational opportunities. The last, and probably most important, aspect of this is the warm hand off to our Marine's first operating force unit. This is a difficult task, but we see too many of our youngest Marines either fall through the cracks or get taken advantage of at this critical point in their Marine Corps experience. This will be the subject of additional communication in the future.

Ground-Based Long-Range Precision Fires

Our investments in air-delivered long-range precision fires (LRPF) are known, suitable, and sufficient; however, we remain woefully behind in the development of ground-based long-range precision-fires that can be fielded in the near term which have sufficient range and precision to deter malign activities or conflict. Our capability development focus has fixated on those capabilities with sufficient range and lethality to support infantry and ground maneuver. This singular focus is no longer appropriate or acceptable. Our ground-based fires must be relevant to the fleet and joint force commanders and provide overmatch against potential adversaries, or they risk irrelevance.

We must develop capabilities to facilitate sea denial and sea control; thus, augmenting the fleet and joint force's use of the sea for our own interests while denying adversaries the same possibilities. These capabilities will facilitate the creation of denied spaces by forward postured or deployed naval expeditionary forces with sufficient resilience to persist within the weapons-engagement-zone (WEZ) once actively contested. We must possess the ability to turn maritime spaces into barriers so we can attack an adversary's sea lines of communication (SLOC) while defending our own in support of the Fleet or Joint Force. This goal requires ground-based LRPF with no less than 350NM ranges – with greater ranges desired. Possession of such capabilities is not only an operational imperative based on the threat, but one that will increase options to commanders, and should radically alter our forward posture once fully realized.

Unmanned Systems

Given well-documented trends in all warfare domains toward increasing range, precision, and lethality of ordnance, ubiquitous multi-spectrum reconnaissance and surveillance, and real-time networked command and control, it is unlikely that exquisite manned platforms represent a complete answer to our needs in future warfare. A likely vision of warfare centers on the recon/counter-recon contest. This demands an agile, stealthy tactical system employing forces that are able to locate, target, and fire precisely first. Exponentially greater precision and lethality of threat weapons demands we reduce exposure of our most expensive platforms and reduce exposure of Marines wherever possible. This means a significant increase in unmanned systems.

This vision, widely discussed since at least the late 1990s, has been slower to arrive than some expected, but gains greater salience as renewed great power competition advances and advanced technology continues to proliferate globally. We have begun adapting to this likely future with tentative and internally-contested steps toward fielding a family of unmanned aerial systems, including the proven long-range, high-endurance armed Group 5 systems that have been ubiquitous in the counter-insurgency warfare of the past decades. We will build upon this progress and work rapidly, starting with POM-22, to develop a much broader family of unmanned systems suitable for reconnaissance, surveillance, and the delivery of lethal and non-lethal effects in the air, on land, and on and under the sea. Development of this family of systems will account for the demands of our role in all phases of a fully integrated naval campaign. **We will prioritize short-term fielding of proven technology, and will significantly increase our efforts to mature unmanned capabilities in other domains.** Mindful that any present vision of the specific nature of future warfare is likely to be flawed, development of our family of unmanned systems will proceed within the framework of a deliberate, fully resourced process of concept development, wargaming, and experimentation. We will meet the inevitable resourcing challenges of experimentation and eventual full fielding as necessary by judicious acceptance of risk and capacity reductions in current capabilities across the force.

C2 in a degraded environment

We have yet to fully develop a robust capability necessary to maintain advantages in the information environment across all seven warfighting functions. This effort will remain a priority for investment and future force development.

Air and Missile Defense (Directed Energy, Counter-Precision Guided Munitions, and Ground-Based Air-Defense)

We must continue to prioritize investments in modern, sophisticated air defense capabilities to include those capabilities which are required by our forward-deployed stand-in forces for persistence inside the adversary WEZ. Regardless of capability enhancements to our overall lethality, if our forward deployed forces are unable to persist inside the WEZ, then they will likely be irrelevant – if not potential liabilities. We are witnessing the emergence of an era of missile warfare, and must ensure our forces possess the capabilities required to mitigate those threats for themselves, the fleet, and joint force. We must expand our research on this issue, and investigate the merits of directed energy capabilities, as well as counter-precision guided munitions (C-PGM) systems for our forward deployed forces.

Artificial Intelligence, Data Science, and Emerging Technology

The Marine Corps confronts an increasingly complex operational environment abroad and a challenging fiscal outlook. The Marine Corps can no longer accept the inefficiencies inherent in antiquated legacy systems that put an unnecessary burden on the warfighters. We do not currently collect the data we need systematically, we lack the processes and technology to make sense of the data we do collect, and we do not leverage the data we have to identify the decision space in manning, training, and equipping the force. Where we have individual leaders and organizations that are trying to adopt the best practices in data science and data analytics, it is often accomplished through the heroic efforts of a few individuals rather than the organized and sustained effort required to transform how we sense, make sense, and act.

We will make strategic investments in data science, machine learning, and artificial intelligence. Initial investments will be focused on challenges we are confronting in talent management, predictive maintenance, logistics, intelligence, and training. In each of those areas, we have significant data ripe for the application of these tool sets. It is not acceptable to waste resources because we lack the investments in infrastructure, processes, and personnel. These investments will be focused on the application of existing systems and tools (COTS and GOTS). We will leverage the investments other Services have made as a fast follower. These tools will empower our existing analytical community to leverage the advanced education investments the Marine Corps is making in the 88XX community.

> *"All of our investments in data science, machine learning, and artificial intelligence are designed to unleash the incredible talent of the individual Marine."*

The authority to operate (ATO) and information assurance (IA) processes must not be allowed to inhibit the adoption of these technologies and processes. **We will leverage the authorities and guidance in the DON business operations plan to accelerate our transformation from disconnected legacy systems to an integrated data architecture that treats data as it should be – a critical resource. If we need additional authorities we will identify the gaps and pursue the necessary changes to instructions or policy.**

In select cases, we will explore investments in decision support tools that leverage data science and artificial intelligence for the tactical commander. These smaller, high impact investments will facilitate experimentation to determine how it can assist our commanders in the field. While the returns on this investment may be exponential, the technology risk is equally high. We will deliberately partner with our Navy counterparts to maximize the investment and share the risks. We are a naval force. Our tactical and operational IA investments will reflect the inherently naval character and the future character of war as specified in the *National Defense Strategy*.

All of our investments in data science, machine learning, and artificial intelligence are designed to unleash the incredible talent of the individual Marine. By automating the tasks that are repetitive, time-consuming, and routine, we will create the space in the schedule to train, educate,

and develop our Marines to the level required by the operational environment. We must set conditions so that the Marines can focus on warfighting tasks rather than data entry and redundant administrative processes. This will make the Marine Corps more lethal. It will also make it easier to recruit and retain the Marines who will be able to excel in the future operating environment.

Divestment Guidance

As we continue to develop our capabilities, we must ensure we have the operationally relevant forces the Combatant Commanders and Fleet Commanders need. It is our responsibility to provide ready forces – forces ready to satisfy Combatant Commander requests for forces. We cannot continue to accept the preservation of legacy capabilities with little to no demand signal, or those that are only being retained in support of surge requirements associated with the least-likely, worst-case scenario. Capabilities and force elements meeting this criteria are candidates for divestment. Such divestitures are necessary so that we may continue to grow our most demanded force elements, to include those that are habitually identified as high-demand, low supply elements within our current Total Obligation Authority (TOA). We cannot allow individuals within the decision-making chain to prevent the procurement of advanced systems and modern capabilities in high demand from our customers due to irrational and empty concerns that "they will be taken from us." As I stated earlier, we provide ready forces, and evidence of the relevance and readiness of our force is customer demand. Furthermore, we will re-scope capabilities and associated force structure in a manner consistent with what is sustainable. We cannot afford to create force structure that our manpower models cannot support.

EDUCATION AND TRAINING

EDUCATION

The complexity of the modern battlefield and increasing rate of change requires a highly educated force. While different, education and training are inextricably linked. Education denotes study and intellectual development. Training is primarily learning-by-doing. We will not train without the presence of education; we must not educate without the complementary execution of well-conceived training. As the 31st Commandant of the Marine Corps noted – "any mission undertaken by the Corps will flow directly from our ability both to train and educate every Marine." In order to meet our desired endstate in education, substantial reforms are required in the organization of our training commands and our formal schools. Appropriate focus on the selection processes is essential to select the right Marines as instructors, trainers, and educators.

As noted by every Commandant since the 29th Commandant of the Marine Corps, our Marines must be comfortable with chaos, comfortable with mission tactics, and comfortable operating in a highly distributed manner across any potential battlefield. While I support this conclusion, I am convinced that attempts to regiment every minute of every day to remove as much friction and potential chaos from the individual Marine while in home-station is counter-productive. We will never create a natural comfort with distributed operations and mission tactics if we continue to impose the most inflexible and overly-structured architecture at home-station. This must change. The continued use of overly hierarchical organizational models must be changed to facilitate the development of the individual Marines and force we need.

Professional Military Education

Few developments within the Marine Corps during my time in service have been more revolutionary than that undertaken in PME – the most important of which were initiated by the 29th Commandant. PME is not something reserved solely for officers; rather, something expected and sought-after by our Non-Commissioned Officers (NCOs) and Staff Non-Commissioned Officers (SNCOs). This is a positive approach; one I will continue to support. PME is the responsibility of every Marine, and takes many forms from individual professional reading to formal school

participation. It is your responsibility to seek PME as part of "self-improvement" and reap the benefits of those educational opportunities provided; I will do everything possible to ensure the policies, resources, infrastructure, and educators are well-established to support you.

I have noticed over the past several years that there is an increasing dissonance between what we are doing with regard to training and education, and what we need to be doing based on the evolving operating environment. Specifically, many of our schools and training venues are firmly based in the "lecture, memorize facts, regurgitate facts on command" model of industrial age training and education. For our schools, it is more about the process of presenting information, and for our students/trainees, it is about what to think and what to do instead of how to think, decide, and act. What we need is an information age approach that is focused on active, student-centered learning using a problem-posing methodology where our students/trainees are challenged with problems that they tackle as groups in order to learn by doing and also from each other. We have to enable them to think critically, recognize when change is needed and inculcate a bias for action without waiting to be told what to do. While I think our officer and enlisted PME systems have made some progress in this area over the past 5-10 years, we need the rest of the Training and Education Command (TECOM) enterprise to catch up.

PME is not a luxury and certainly not a reward for previous accomplishment or service; but rather, a necessary investment by the service to facilitate readiness across the force. We must cease viewing PME as something less strenuous and less challenging than other tours of service, and seek to make it as competitive and rewarding as possible. I am committed to ensuring each of you is provided the best educational opportunity available; however, I am also committed to ensuring that the opportunity is as academically rigorous as possible, and no longer consequence free. This will require changes in how we evaluate academic performance, as well as how we annotate success, mediocrity, and potentially failure via performance evaluations. We must expect a greater return on our investments from the $50,000 per student cost, for example, at Command and Staff College. That experience must result in greater identification of the most and least talented individuals.

Naval Education

As a service, we lack the requisite naval education to engage our fellow naval officers and peers constructively in discussions on naval concepts, naval programs, or naval warfare. While we can and should take pride in our ability to develop a deep reservoir of knowledge on counterinsurgency operations, we must now direct our attention and energy to replicating that educational effort across the force to create a similar knowledge base regarding naval warfare and naval expeditionary warfare. **All our formal schools must and will change their programs of instruction to include a greater naval orientation.** We must all have a better understanding of composite warfare and the JFMCC as a whole. To that end, I will direct all of our Brigadier Generals and Brigadier General-selects to attend the Navy JFMCC Course along with their Navy peers.

Learning

We must invest robustly in wargaming, experimentation, and modeling & simulation (M&S) if we are to be a successful learning organization. **The National Defense Strategy has directed us to focus in new areas, and this requires us to think, innovate, and change.** Addressing these new missions starts with ideas, ideas are developed into concepts, and concepts that are then tested and refined by wargaming, experimentation, and M&S.

We are currently imbalanced across these learning activities. We have applied substantial energies to developing new concepts over the last two decades, but our "proofing" of these concepts through rigorous wargaming, experimentation, and analysis has been inadequate. Such activities are essential if we are going to translate our concepts into action. We have a poor transition record in this regard, and our lack of sufficient analysis and experimentation is a major factor contributing to this deficiency.

It is obvious from our concept development work that significant change is required in how we organize, train, and equip our Corps for the future. Innovation will be critical, but it is in the actual implementation of our innovative concepts that we will be judged. For the Marine Corps, meaningful innovation is not just having great thoughts and concepts rather, it is about translating great thoughts and concepts into action.

Our PPBE process by which we determine how we spend our resources will be driven by a planning phase informed by wargaming, modeling and simulation, and build on a solid analytic foundation closely integrated with the Navy. We must invest more in these learning activities.

Finally, we need a doctrinal publication to formulate how Marines will learn in the years ahead and why it is so important that they "buy in" to the concept. It needs to set the groundwork firmly in adult learning methodology with an emphasis on teamwork, problem solving, and enabling the ability for all of our Marines to cycle through the OODA (Observe, Orient, Decide, Act) loop faster than any opponent we may face with a bias for intelligent action becoming second nature to all Marines.

TRAINING

We should train the way we expect and intend to fight. If we expect to operate in a contested information environment, then we will train to that standard and expectation. If we expect to operate in an environment in which losing the hider-finder competition will result in attack by mass indirect fires, then we will train that way. If we anticipate operating in distributed naval and expeditionary formations due to the ascendancy of missile warfare, then we will train that way. We must adapt our training in a manner consistent with the threat and anticipated operational challenges. If we will be required to create mutually contested maritime spaces, then we must train to do so. If we will be required to persist inside an advanced adversary's WEZ, then we must train to do so. If we anticipate a requirement to seize and defend, then we must train to do so, regardless of obstacles such as non-availability of amphibious ships.

As with our formal schools, we must enforce a more disciplined and rigorous assessment model in which not every unit passes, and for which there are both rewards and punishments for performance. We must be able to say with confidence that the $5.5M we expend per ITX rotation is causing greater readiness and, therefore, providing a return to the service for the investment.

Training must be focused on winning in combat in the most challenging conditions and operating environments – from the thin air and high altitudes of the mountains, to the sweltering heat of triple canopy jungles, and including the sprawling self-organized chaos of dense urban terrain. Marines must be comfortable operating in all potential environments. Wherever possible, training will be progressive and practical in nature. We must make the most of every learning opportunity in garrison before units go to the field. Training must include appropriate background reading, tactical decision games, modeling and simulations, and augmented reality. Everything should be subject to a formal critique, which is a particularly important part of performance oriented training.

WARGAMING

Essential to charting our course in an era of strategic fluidity and rapid change will be the effective integration of professional wargaming in force design, education, and training. Often conflated in the minds of some Marines with recreational pastimes, or perhaps more often with simulations used for individual and small unit training, wargaming is in fact a set of tools for structured thinking about military problems within a competitive framework – in the presence of that "thinking enemy" who lies at the heart of our doctrinal understanding of war. Successful military innovations of the past, from our own naval services' development of amphibious warfare doctrine to Tukhachevsky's formulation of "Deep Battle," rested on a foundation of properly-integrated wargaming. As with other aspects of our current performance, our problem is not that we are not doing wargaming – indeed, we have something of a proliferation of entities engaged in the practice – but that we have not effectively harnessed this effort in an integrated process of learning generating tangible, defensible results. This will change.

We will build a Wargaming Center on the Marine Corps University (MCU) campus. The most important aspect of this project will be hiring the right people to operate the facility. While the facility must be able to handle all levels of classification and be responsive to changing technologies, our biggest investment will be maintaining the right technical and non-technical personnel. We will need experts in wargaming, M&S, facilitation, threats, and opportunities.

Marine Corps Warfighting Lab

The 31st Commandant established the Marine Corps Warfighting Laboratory (MCWL) "to serve as the cradle and test bed for the development of enhanced operational concepts, tactics, techniques, procedures, and doctrine which will be progressively introduced into the FMF in concert with new technologies." Over the years, the Lab's structure and mission have evolved. Given the pace and consequence of on-going technological change, the Lab must continue to evolve to meet the demands of the future strategic and operational environment.

Our Lab will serve as the focal point and integrating ground for new concepts, capabilities, and technologies that we develop, as well as a key enabler for accelerating the Service's future force development efforts. The Lab will continue to prioritize the development of naval concepts and capabilities, and Fleet Marine Force support to naval campaigns.

To accomplish these objectives, some change is required. To ensure investment in critical 'leap ahead technologies', the MCWL shall be responsible for providing recommendations to DC CD&I and the MROC for a dedicated slice of the Warfighting Investment Program Evaluation Board (WIPEB). Once we have addressed these resource shortfalls and updated responsibility for WIPEB investment recommendations that prioritize modernization, the Lab will be responsible for development, field testing, and implementation of future operational and functional concepts, along with supporting technologies, as well as for working across the enterprise to accelerate potential DOTMLPF changes.

While the OPFOR's role in support of Service-level experimentation is essential, we will have only one integrated Service-level wargaming and experimentation campaign led by the Warfighting Laboratory. Other entities across the enterprise and OPFOR will cease any non-integrated effort with MCWL's larger experimentation campaign. This is not intended to stifle experimentation and innovation; but instead, to create focus with our limited resources. MCWL will continue to rely on the OPFOR – for their best and most innovative minds – to achieve success.

Wargaming in Force Design

The vehicle for change, in terms of wargaming in support of force design, will be the MCWL. A major focus of my tenure as Commandant will be my direct, personal, regular engagement with our Warfighting Laboratory to drive an integrated process of wargaming and experimentation that will rapidly produce solutions for further development in accordance with my guidance and vision. That vision centers on three conceptual foundations mentioned above – *Distributed Operations*, *Littoral Operations in a Contested Environment*, and *Expeditionary Advanced Base Operations*. The Marine Corps' role in these concepts is inseparable from the broad sweep of naval operations; accordingly, we should think in terms of their execution within the framework of the Navy's *Composite Warfare* doctrine. We will ensure that a single wargaming entity within MCWL proceeds systematically, and rapidly, through a series of games designed to explore the implications of the designated concepts in specific, real-world scenarios based on the current NDS, *National Military Strategy* (NMS), and other relevant departmental guidance. This wargaming effort will be the centerpiece of my effort to generate reliable knowledge upon which to base force design and combat development.

Resourcing a real "campaign of learning" presents challenges. It cannot be done simply by tasking existing organizations to do what they are inclined to do already. Inherent in our rhetoric of renewed great power competition in an era of exponential technological and social change is the understanding that accepting risk in current capability, before emerging threats fully mature, is a reasonable price to pay for a better chance of properly anticipating future requirements. Further guidance on resourcing will follow, but deliberate service-level O-6 and O-5 talent management, permanent manning adjustments, fiscal reprogramming, and the temporary allocation of highly-qualified manpower from the MCU student population, are all elements of a likely solution for proper resourcing of this critical effort.

Wargaming in Education and Training

In the context of training, wargaming needs to be used more broadly to fill what is arguably our greatest deficiency in the training and education of leaders: practice in decision-making against a thinking enemy. Again, this requirement is inherent in the nature of war. In modern military organizations, it is, along with the fear of violent death, precisely the element of real war that is hardest to replicate under peacetime conditions. Wargaming historically was invented to fill this gap, and we need to make far more aggressive use of it at all levels of training and education to give leaders the necessary "reps and sets" in realistic combat decision-making. In particular, the spectrum of larger unit training, focused on commanders and staffs at battalion/squadron and higher levels, remains tightly focused on standardized tactics, techniques, and procedures and deals too little with the challenge of making the tactical decisions, under stress, that these TTP exist to implement. Large unit exercises, from MEF-level command post exercises to battalion-focused Integrated Training Exercises, must focus primarily on commanders' decision-making under conditions of uncertainty and their staffs' ability to support such decisions, and only secondarily on the TTP of combined-arms integration and technical command and control. This is a tall order, as the latter are obviously the essential building blocks of the

former. However, we must make this shift. Available technology is likely to offer potential solutions if we refine what we are asking of it: we need less of the grand "simulations" solution connecting a variety of individual cockpit or rifleman-level sims into the flow of larger exercises than a modernized command and control system that integrates advanced wargaming functions for both training and planning. Clearly, potential exists for synergy between MCU's educational wargaming, MCWL's wargaming efforts in support of force design, and the requirements for increased use of wargaming in tactical training. We will pursue such opportunities with determination and energy.

> *"Our wargames have shown that in any great power conflict, our alliances are an essential factor to achieving success."*

Wargaming Findings

In alignment with strategic guidance, our Service-level wargames over the past few years have focused on warfighting scenarios involving peer adversaries. The insights from these wargames inform future force development and indicate a requirement to adapt our concepts and capabilities for waging great power competition and conflict. We have Service initiatives already in motion that position us for change. In February of 2019, the Commandant and Chief of Naval Operations co-signed the concept for EABO. The ideas contained in this document are foundational to our future force development efforts and are applicable in multiple scenarios. While our Corps' history provides numerous examples of similar type operations, we now need new capabilities if we are to implement EABO in its full scope in a future conflict against the pacing threat.

Our wargames have shown that in any great power conflict, our alliances are an essential factor to achieving success. We will fight in defense of our allies and will operate in close alignment with them, from their territories, alongside their ships and aircraft, and in cooperative and even integrated formations on the ground. We must work with them in peace to be ready to partner with them in war. Our forward deployed forces will continue to enhance the interoperability of our tactics, techniques, and procedures, while our capability developers enhance the interoperability of our systems.

To succeed in closing the force in any future conflict, we must re-imagine our amphibious ship capabilities, prepositioning, and expeditionary logistics so they are more survivable, at less risk of catastrophic loss, and agile in their employment. We must add sensors and defensive systems to our current fleet of amphibious ships while we explore alternative future platforms, amphibious operations concepts, and evolved Marine Expeditionary Unit configurations. We must leverage the strategic re-capitalization of our Maritime Prepositioning Ship Squadrons to develop smaller and more versatile ships. We also need to explore ocean going connectors that enable our intra-theater movement and sustainment.

Our wargaming, analysis, and real-world operations show that advancements in technologies across all domains enhance situational awareness and long-range precision strike, not only for us but also for our peer adversaries. In any future conflict, we will face challenges in maneuvering and operating inside threat weapons engagement zones. We must be prepared to counter threat sensors at operational and tactical levels. And we must have capabilities that enable the MAGTF to sense and strike across all domains.

Critical to warfighting success in environments characterized by distributed operations across wide expanses of battlespace is an effective and resilient command and control system. Our communications nodes will be hunted and targeted. Careless and unmanaged signatures will invite destruction. We require interoperable, low signature, secure communications. We cannot develop this in isolation from the other Services. We must be capable of plugging into naval, joint, and combined communications networks and seamlessly sharing data that enhances situational awareness, targeting, and force synchronization.

Autonomous systems and artificial intelligence are rapidly changing the character of war. We have already seen these changes on today's battlefields, but we are only at the leading edge of revolutionary changes. Our potential peer adversaries are investing heavily to gain dominance in these fields. We must aggressively research, innovate, and adapt to maximize the potential these offer while mitigating their inherent vulnerabilities and risks. Our wargames and experiments have shown game-changing opportunities with manned and unmanned teaming.

At the forward tactical edge of the FMF are our F-35s, reconnaissance teams, and rifle squads. This combined arms triad of warriors imbued with our warfighting ethos, integrated with and enhanced by unmanned sensors and weapons platforms, and enabled by the combat support and combat service support functions of the FMF, can be a dominating and decisive force on any battlefield against any adversary. We must leverage unmanned technologies and artificial intelligence to enhance our situational awareness, lethality, and expeditionary potential.

Some specific technologies our wargames have shown to be of particular importance are long-range unmanned surface vessels (LRUSV) as sensors, weapons, and sustainment platforms; ground based long-range precision fires capabilities that can strike moving targets in both land and sea domains; high-endurance loitering sensors and munitions employable from the squad to MEF levels; advanced air defense capabilities; and low probability of intercept (LPI) / low probability of detection (LPD) communications and radars. Integrating these capabilities, and others, will entail significant force structure changes and development of new concepts of employment across the MAGTF.

CORE VALUES - HONOR, COURAGE, COMMITMENT

CULTURE

The Marine Corps developed its warfighting spirit and character in the values of honor, courage, and commitment. The sentiment these concepts evoke are seen and felt in the shared experiences, hardships, and challenges in training and combat and embody what it is to be a Marine – they cannot be mandated, yet live in the collective soul of our Corps. **Our rich history demonstrates this ethos and has led generations of Marines to success on and off the battlefield.**

Non-EAS Attrition

The continued loss of 8,000 Marines per year to non-EAS attrition is unacceptable. According to Manpower and Reserve Affairs (M&RA), between FY09-19, the OPFOR lost 11,765 Marines to non-EAS attrition for drug and alcohol offenses, and another 13,571 for misconduct. The total replacement cost for these 25,336 Marines is in excess of $1 billion. This must change.

> *"The Marine Corps developed its warfighting spirit and character in the values of honor, courage, and commitment."*

"The soul of the Marine Corps," as previously noted by Commandant Barrow, is sound. While sound, this does not mean we should ever neglect it or assume it will persist without consistent and purposeful reflection and active cultivation. **We are an elite institution of warriors, and will remain so on my watch.** It is our shared responsibility to ensure the continued health of our collective soul and identity.

Sexual Assault

Sexual Assault remains the most troubling destructive behavior to me. Despite the best efforts of individual leaders across the force, the continued rise in reporting leads me to conclude that we still do not fully understand the scope and scale of the issue, or that we can say with any confidence that the measures we have taken to-date are preventing sexual assaults. I am committed to the position that the unit commander should remain involved in the process and disposition of cases, yet recognize additional steps are required. We will emphasize the need to educate the force in areas such as unconscious bias. We will focus on prevention, victim protection and legal support, and timely completion of investigations. **Sexual assault is a crime, and Marines found guilty of committing sexual assault will be held accountable.**

Drug Use

I remain troubled by the extent to which drug abuse is a characteristic of new recruits, and the fact the vast majority of recruits require drug waivers for enlistment. I am equally troubled by the fact that we do not specifically monitor personnel for continued substance abuse while in-service. Finally, I am deeply troubled by the continued retention of Marines failing to adhere to our standards related to drug use. Since the beginning of FY18, 2,410 Marines have tested positive for illegal drug use; yet, only 1,175 (48.8%) have been separated.

Hazing

All destructive behavior concerns me, and the eradication of that misconduct will be a priority for me; yet, I am very troubled by hazing. While I believe hazing is likely underreported, during the most recent four-year period we have witnessed a significant increase in both reports and substantiated reports of hazing. Hazing is both a crime and evidence of poor leadership by our SNCOs and Officers. We place special trust and confidence in our SNCOs and Officers, and any who engage in hazing will be held accountable.

COMMAND AND LEADERSHIP

As Commandant, I am responsible for the selection of the best and fully qualified commanders. Those selected for command have earned our special trust and confidence and are accountable for all decisions and actions. When commanders fail to measure up to standards, they will be held accountable.

Leaders must ensure Marines are well-led and cared for physically, emotionally, and spiritually, both in and out of combat. "Taking care of Marines" means vigorously enforcing our high standards of performance and conduct, it does not mean relaxing the standard. When we fail to hold the standard, we establish new lower standards. Elite organizations do not accept mediocrity and they do not look the other way when teammates come up short of expectations. We must hold each other accountable.

There is no place in our Marine Corps for those who deliberately misuse their authority to physically or sexually assault another; no place for those who risk the lives of those they seek to serve by operating a motor vehicle while impaired; no place for those who are intolerant of their fellow Marines' gender or sexual orientation; no place for those who engage in domestic violence; and no place for racists – whether their intolerance and prejudice be direct or indirect, intentional or unintentional.

In some organizations, internal problems are often elevated to the most senior levels or down to the most junior ranks for corrective action. For the Marine Corps, our company grade officers and mid-grade SNCOs have the appropriate experience base, maturity, and daily interactions with junior Marines. Those leaders have my full faith and confidence. I know they are fully capable of balancing a sincere concern for their Marines well-being with an unwavering demand to adhere to our high standards. They must be allowed to lead without unnecessary interference and micro-management.

For our officer corps, I require that you provide every opportunity for your junior officers and enlisted leaders to lead, educate, train, supervise, and enforce high standards. Do not encroach on their space unnecessarily and do not prescribe every action; instead, teach, coach, and mentor. Our maneuver warfare doctrine depends on commander's intent and mission-type orders – we must train how we fight.

"Taking care of Marines" means vigorously enforcing our high standards of performance and conduct, it does not mean relaxing the standard.

SUMMARY

This CPG establishes my priorities for aligning the Service with the NDS and DPG; enhancing our warfighting capability through naval integration; achieving the proper balance of resources in our readiness, modernization, and infrastructure sustainment efforts and accounts; and improving the quality of leadership we provide our Marines and Sailors.

While not all encompassing, this CPG is thorough to provide clear guidance on the way forward. I expect all Marines, and particularly senior officers and Staff Non-Commissioned Officers, to read and begin implementing this guidance immediately. Within the next 30 days, the Director of the Marine Corps Staff, will publish a detailed implementation plan to accompany this guidance. That plan will identify specified and implied tasks derived from the CPG, the command or office of primary responsibility, and timelines. Your continued feedback and ideas on this document and the full range of issues affecting our Corps are critical.

We are entering a period of force transformation, one through which I am honored to lead our Corps. This CPG identifies those characteristics and capabilities within the force that must change to produce the force we must become to meet the challenges of the NDS and uncertainty of the future operating environment. We will not employ these in isolation, and thus we must better integrate with the Navy and work more effectively with other elements of the Joint Force. While this transformation will require more than simply the next four years, as maneuverists we are prepared to make bold decisions more rapidly than others to effect those outcomes, to generate tempo, and create friction within the decision cycles of our competitors and adversaries.

While the next four years will be a period of substantive change – let me be clear – we are not experiencing an identity crisis nor are we at risk of irrelevance. **We are a naval expeditionary force capable of deterring malign behavior and, when necessary, fighting inside our adversary's weapons-engagement-zone to facilitate sea denial in support of fleet operation and joint force horizontal escalation.** Nothing could be more relevant to the NDS and the certainty of an uncertain future than this. We are not a second land army, nor do we aspire to be anything other than the world's premier naval expeditionary force. While these are intended as statements of fact and conclusions vice empty assertions, our actions haven't always supported our statements. This will change. As we implement the guidance in this document, we must divest of the past to modernize for the future – and we will.

In the summer of 2023, when we anticipate a routine transition to a new Commandant, we will have accomplished the following, at a minimum:

- Designed the Marine Corps of the next 25 years as prescribed in the NDS, NMS, DPG, and as further visualized in our family of naval concepts. This design effort includes making the necessary divestments from the current force and current program to accelerate the funding and modernization of the future force.

- Re-established our identity as a naval expeditionary force, and enhanced our relationship with the Fleets as an extension of naval power as the FMF.

- Re-established our primacy within the Department as the most innovative and revolutionary thinkers, the most well-disciplined and accountable force, and the most transparent and responsive force to our collective civilian leadership across the Joint Force and Department.

It is an exciting time to be a Marine. Strategic guidance casts the Marine Corps in a central role in our Nation's defense, and this planning guidance is designed to ensure our Corps is prepared for this responsibility. The initiatives outlined in this document identify my priorities for improving the quality of the leadership we provide the Marines and Sailors, enhancing our warfighting capability and naval integration, and achieving the proper allocation of resources across readiness, modernization, and personnel accounts.

Ensuring a shared understanding of this guidance is a shared responsibility, and I expect unit commanders and senior leaders to ensure a broad understanding of this guidance across the force. As important, I expect Marines to be prepared to provide their leaders – me included – with critical feedback, ideas, and perspective on this CPG. Bringing about the changes outlined in this document will be an all-hands effort. We cannot afford to continue to admire problems or fail to take the necessary decisive actions; our strategic guidance is clear, and so is mine. The time for action is now.

Semper Fidelis,

David H. Berger
General, U.S. Marine Corps
Commandant of the Marine Corps

www.ingramcontent.com/pod-product-compliance
Lightning Source LLC
Chambersburg PA
CBHW050618110426
42813CB00008B/2602